CW01654361

UNCONSCIOUS BIAS

How to positively change recruitment, retention, promotion, and career-development within your organisation

DIAN CAMPBELL

ISBN: 978-1-5272-9110-2

First published 2021

Disclaimer

Contents

Acknowledgements

I would like to thank my parents, my beloved father, who is no longer with us, but the unwavering support, I still miss. The encouragement and support from family and friends to write the book. Finally, the support from my husband and sons in encouraging me through the positive challenge in writing this book.

“You may not control all the events that happen to you, but you can decide not to be reduced by them.”

– Maya Angelou

Thank you for buying this book. I hope you find it informative and uplifting. To access a free leaflet on measures to assist in developing and implementing equal career opportunities in organisations, please contact me at:

campbelldc956@gmail.com

Author's note

When I set out to write this book, I thought I had a strong idea of what "unconscious bias" meant, and how it manifests in society. During the research and writing of the content, I have discovered that the divisions in our society in fact run much deeper than I ever could have envisioned. By exploring the lived experiences of a collective group of diverse, underrepresented individuals, *Unconscious Bias* shows the real-world impact of historical prejudice, how it impacts fairness and equality in the workplace, and how it changes everyday life.

Unconscious Bias is an opportunity for reflection, not just for those who have suffered but for those who may have unintentionally discriminated against others in the past. Throughout this book, I have shared the words of wisdom bestowed to me by my parents, who valued hard work and education, and saw the potential in each of their children. My parents were determined that no amount of prejudice or bias would hold their children back, that we would succeed even in the face of societal discrimination. However, this in itself betrays the problem. Equal opportunity shouldn't have to be earned, fought for, or sought after; it should simply **be**.

I sincerely hope that my reflections, thoughts, and analysis can help to make positive changes to your professional and personal life. Unconscious judgement has a lasting impact. But, there is a solution, and this book is filled with ideas on how we—as a society—can bring about positive change, equitable opportunities, equality, and fairness. It starts with you, dear reader. As the saying goes: be the change you want to see.

INTRODUCTION

Hello and thank you for picking up this book. My name is Dian Campbell, before we begin please allow me to tell you a bit about myself:

I have been a social worker for 20 years now, and I have spent the majority of this time working with children and their families, where I have held first-line management positions. Alongside this, I've also worked in marketing and under-writing. As a black female, I've never been afraid of taking on challenges and stepping outside my comfort zone, and with this in mind, it's fair to say that my approach is very 'to the point'. Throughout this book, I will provide you with my own 'to the point' tips and advice to empower and help employers improve their quality of recruitment and retention.

Growing up, my parents supported us children by instilling in us how important getting a good education and working hard is for achieving our goals and aspirations. Actually, their mantra was ‘one could achieve most things in life by working hard.’

My parents left good and stable employment to relocate to the UK, from the Caribbean. They shared with us their experiences of how cold the UK was in both the temperature and the welcome they received when they arrived. We heard their experiences of trying to gain accommodation and the conditions when they eventually found a landlord who would rent to them. The accommodation they described as being very poor but they accepted it as they had no other choice at the time. Acquiring employment was problematic for my parents too, but they were resilient and when they obtained employment, they worked hard holding down several jobs. They saved using the Paadna scheme (*a collective saving scheme popular among the Afro-Caribbean community in the UK since the days of the Windrush, Contributoria.com)*. The Paadna was a lever to help my parents achieve their goals, as at that time securing a bank loan was virtually impossible.

Following years of saving, my parents were able to purchase a large three-storey Victorian house in the 1960s where we lived. They also rented accommodation to two families who were family friends from

Jamaica. These families had experienced tough and unpleasant experiences trying to rent suitable accommodation too. The house would be a home to the families for as long as they needed, which I remember was great, they were like my extended family. This type of support was not unique to my parent's situation, it was replicated by other families who made the journey to the UK for a better life.

My parent's resilience paid off, as my father passed The Black Cab knowledge test first time, which he was very proud of. He owned two taxis, the second he rented at a reasonable price to help his fellow drivers; it was important to my father to be self-employed. My mother was a trained hairdresser and owned a salon and hair-dressing school in Brixton, I remember the annual celebration event when students graduated. She did this for several years, before retraining to become a social worker working with children and then going on to own children's homes.

My parents' guidance about working hard and getting an education to achieve and fulfil my aspirations have been discussed with my friends who received similar advice from their parents. We concluded that our parents wanting the best for us, truly believed in the advice they gave; they were fully aware of prejudice and discrimination but thought this could be overcome by effort and hard work, because of what they achieved.

I initially thought about writing a book on the subject of unconscious bias about two years ago. At the time, unconscious bias did not appear to be openly talked about; however, this has changed, and I welcome the now open discussion taking place. The discussion is long overdue particularly in the workplace which is the area of focus of the book.

There have been interviews on the radio and many television productions on the subject of unconscious bias, with celebrities and everyday folk, sharing their life experiences and talking about solutions for change. A powerful Channel 4 documentary, I watched on the subject was based in a high school where students were split into racial groups for an activity. One particular exercise involved the students taking part in a running race but black children were placed in starting positions at the back, brown children a little way forward, and white students starting at the front. They were placed in positions, based on the answer to questions with black children having experienced more of the microaggressions and discriminations which contributed to them having a starting place further back. It was a simple exercise with such a powerful message. The students got the message straight away, by expressing their views about the unfairness of the race, which they realised reflected real life for the black and brown fellow students.

My view is that the television production mentioned above should be a fundamental part of the school curriculum so young people are aware of how one's skin colour is perceived by some and the impact this can have on one's life. I also think the great take away from the programme, is that we need to equip and inform young people as they are, the panacea for change in challenging inequality moving forward.

"Teaching Black History not only benefits Black and ethnic minority students, but it is also beneficial to British society as a whole.
The cognition which ensues, allows us as a nation to collectively pause and critically reflect on race relations. Widening the scope of Black History study can also help society to unravel and unlearn many of the racial stereotypes (and intergenerational trauma) that linger into the present."

- The Black Curriculum

So, has unconscious bias affected me? And what is the link between the guidance and advice from my parents of working hard to achieve one's goals?

Overall, my career progression has been good, I have been aspirational, honed my craft by working hard, but on reflection, I do feel there have been missed opportunities to progress further and potential left unfulfilled. Throughout my career in social work, I have received positive feedback on the contributions and value I have added in my roles. I also received encouragement from senior and line managers to push for career progression, which I did on a number of occasions. However, these experiences did not result in progression to the next level, although feeling abled and ready for new career challenges. Clearly, some will question interview performances, but the subsequent chapters, will explore examples of similar experiences, experienced by black workers.

I secured a position as an interim manager, senior to a first-line manager role. The location of the job meant working away from home for the week. It became obvious that I could not sustain the working arrangements and ended the contract after about five months, the feedback was positive and reinforced my belief in my capabilities.

That said, I was excited to start writing the book to explore these issues in more depth and hear experiences from colleagues and friends about work experiences in their respective organisations. I wanted to further consider the potential impact on individuals if they felt they had experienced unconscious bias. Finally, the aim of the book is to reflect on how we recognise and identify unconscious bias. I provide constructive suggestions and measures on changes, in my opinion, that are needed, to benefit both employees and employers on issues of diversity, recruitment, retention and career development.

Chapter 1

The impact of unconscious bias

"It is not our differences that divide us.
It is our inability to recognize, accept,
and celebrate those differences."

- Audre Lorde

The aim of this chapter is to examine the impact of unconscious bias and reflect on where we are now. Solutions are also considered with the goal being fairness with equal opportunities. In the introduction, I talked about my reason for writing this book on unconscious bias from my perspective about race. However, I am acutely aware, that unconscious bias can be experienced by other sectors of society, some of these relate to one's gender, age, disability, and sexual orientation. The point is that there are different ways in which unconscious bias can affect people's lives. The principles in this book can be applied to anyone from a minority background or protected characteristic.

Banaji and Greenwald offer a helpful definition of unconscious bias:

> *Banaji and Greenwald (2013) likened unconscious bias to the blind spot in the retina. The difference is that we are able to "see" our blind spot by looking at a specially marked piece of paper and covering one eye. Unfortunately, our unconscious biases operate as hidden blind spots, ones that are difficult to see and of which we are unaware yet influence our beliefs about and behavior toward others. Banaji and Greenwald defined unconscious biases as acquired "bits of knowledge about social groups" (p. xii) that implicitly and automatically shape our thoughts and responses to*

others in both positive and negative ways. They note that most of us are "good people" who are generally well intentioned and try to behave in ways consistent with our good intentions, and who usually resist the very idea that we hold such biases. Even more so, we especially resist the notion that our unconscious biases influence our behaviour toward others.

Unconscious bias is intrinsically linked to stereotypical beliefs individuals hold which can be based on beliefs held by family and friends, the historical portrayal of black people as submissive, and questions about their intellectual ability being inferior to their white counterparts.

Black people, especially black males, are portrayed negatively in the media. This has carried over into the entertainment sector as in movies and in television, black people are often cast in roles as drug dealers, gangsters, and other crime-related occupations. While we have seen a positive change with black directors and producers, I believe portrayals in entertainment and the media described above, can cause people to create their own depictions and assumptions on what black culture really is.

The education system is fundamental in shaping the learning and understanding of the involvement of black and ethnic minorities in the economic and social contribution to the United Kingdom. The knowledge of educators and their confidence to teach the subject of diversity is of equal importance, as noted in the quote below:

Britain's diverse and multi-cultural history does not only hinge upon the content taught to pupils, but perhaps of equal importance, is how teachers are supported pedagogically and professionally to teach diverse curricula effectively, accurately and confidently (Alexander & Arday, 2015; D'Avray et al., 2013).

Stereotypical views manifest themselves in ways that are harmful and damaging. They not only hurt the feelings of black people and ethnic minorities but they also deprive them of positive interactions with white people because they do not value their contributions or see them as equal.

We need to acknowledge that there are likely to be people who hold these harmful views, that may not be aware that they do. This could be a result of views held in their subconscious mind, which influence their actions and feelings towards others. I heard an interesting study being discussed on the radio about the unconscious mind. The study was set in a lecture theatre of approximately one hundred white and two black students. The lecturers focused on the black students giving them more eye contact and seemingly viewed that they required more attention. There may be a number of reasons why the lecturers focused on the two black students in this way, but it appears there was something in their unconsciousness, which led the lectures to focus their attention on the two black students. Interestingly, when later discussed with the lecturers they all stated that they were not aware they were doing this. Following reflection on this study, I wonder what the thoughts and feelings were of the two students, being placed in the spotlight in this way?

It is important to have spaces where we can hold difficult conversations about biases held to understand their origin and ultimately, help change these views. To appreciate and recognise the positives in difference, in my opinion, can only enrich the organisation's embracement of diversity.

Below are examples of unconscious bias I have experienced:

Example 1

I had a telephone discussion with a professional and at the end of the call we agreed the way forward was to convene a meeting for all professionals to attend to discuss the next steps. Some of the attendees I had met previously, but I hadn't met the professional I had held the telephone discussion with. I greeted the professionals as they arrived and the person, I spoke to on the phone introduced herself and I said, "Oh yes, we spoke on the phone." Unfortunately, before she was able to stop herself the expression on her face gave away what I knew she was thinking and out it came, "I did not expect to…"

I said, "Who were you expecting?" She babbled something and took her seat. This is not the first time I have experienced this;

I have encountered this before where I have been told that I don't have an accent, and have even been told I don't sound like a black person! I think the assumption by some is that all black people should be speaking 'patois'.

Example 2

People have had a strange fascination with my hair. I say strange because it is what I was born with and I didn't understand the interest, as my hair defines me and I love it. But over the years, in different scenarios, I have received comments suggesting that my hair looks like cotton wool and get asked if it feels like cotton wool. Still, to this day, I get asked by people if they can touch my hair. This happens when I'm out shopping, in exercise classes, and at work and this list is in no way exhaustive. My point here is that it happens a lot! People appear offended and surprised when the offer to touch my hair is declined. I am usually viewed as unnecessarily irritated by the request!

At school, I accepted that there were curiosities from peers about my hair and understood that this is how we learn from each other, so while I was frustrated at school with requests to touch my hair, I didn't have the forethought to think it would continue into adulthood!

Examples below were shared by colleagues over the years:

Example 3

As a manager, I attended a meeting which I was chairing, with me was a white colleague whom I managed and was supporting. I had not met the meeting attendees previously. Before the meeting started and we had the opportunity for introductions, one of the meeting attendees preceded to direct questions to my colleague who responded by saying you will need to ask my manager and turned to me. The attendee apologised for the assumption made and while someone may say that was an easy mistake to make, it is interesting that something in the attendee's subconscious led her to make the assumption, on who she felt had the capability, knowledge, or authority to respond.

Example 4

I was told by a white colleague that as a black male my appearance was threatening and intimidating, this was said without any prior interaction with the white female. I was concerned by the comment. Unconscious bias was clearly evident but I would also go as far as to say the comments were racist. I reflected on the comments which were likely based on stereotypical views e.g., black males associated with hostility, aggression, and belonging to gangs. What is also concerning with this example is the lack of understanding of the negative impact and offence regarding the comments made.

Example 5

This example was while listening to a question-and-answer session on a radio station. black women called the station to share their experience during childbirth. One of the themes of the experiences was the restriction in getting pain relief. This was based on the perception of some medics that black women have a high pain threshold. This was dispelled by the medic on the show but nevertheless, an experience, experienced by callers to the show.

By providing these real-life examples of unconscious bias, I want to encourage individuals to reflect on their behaviours and assumptions that impact negatively on black people. I am not in a position nor is it my place to speak for all black people, but while I have developed a good protective armour over the years, I would be being dishonest, if I didn't say I find it wearing to encounter the examples described above. I am very proud of my race and heritage and it is disappointing that some people see this as a barrier to getting to know me as a person and others who encounter similar experiences.

Ways to combat and change stereotypical views are possible but it may not be an easy process to change negative views held about someone who is perceived as different. The impact of people holding racist views are worrying but what is more concerning is when that person influences one's aspirations to career progression. Working harder and doing more to demonstrate your abilities may not be enough to break through the glass ceiling, because assumptions and judgements which appear not to be based on your ability but your race hold you back.

The matter is complex because unconscious bias can be subtle in that it's difficult to prove. Over the years, I have experienced interactions that have not exactly been positive, and I have been left perplexed as to the justification of the behaviour. Trying to challenge or address these interactions is problematic as one may be perceived as being oversensitive or conflating a situation. I think this is linked to a reluctance to tackle a wider issue and the view that it is probably easier to minimise the concerning behaviour which leaves the matter unresolved.

Over the years, I have worked and encountered positive working relationships, but creating space for dialogue without blame, is fundamental in understanding differing perspectives, as by the very nature of the term someone may be unaware of biases held. We are susceptible to the trap of forming an opinion about someone we've met for the first time. Critically, the danger arises when individuals in powerful positions unconsciously use their beliefs in a manner that negatively impacts an underrepresented employee's ability to achieve.

Chapter 2
The status quo

"It is time for parents to teach young people early on that in diversity there is beauty and there is strength. We all should know that diversity makes for a rich tapestry, and we must understand that all the threads of that tapestry are equal in value no matter their color."

Maya Angelou

This chapter builds on chapter 1 but also explores the barriers within organisations in embracing diversity and equality in the workforce.

Unconscious biases serve as "social mindbugs" (Banaji & Greenwald, 2013, p. 13). These are contextual cues that lead us to form unconscious social inferences that influence how we perceive and behave toward people from social groups that are alike or different from our own. Noting that "the mind forms strong alliances with things and people that are familiar while developing subtle biases against those that aren't," Ives Erickson (2015) pointed out "these biases exist in our minds without our knowledge or consent" (p. 2).

The quote by Ives Erickson (2015) is interesting, as it may be a factor when recruiting managers fill a vacancy with someone who they have a strong alliance or social group they identify with. Could this practice, also be linked to a bias based on fear of difference? Whatever the reason, doing this is not equitable and failing to utilise the talent of underrepresented workers.

How an organisation operates and its behaviour over time e.g., governance, staff makeup, and culture correlates with the values of the decision-makers and leaders. For example, senior Leaders need to be confident that the organisation's ethos, e.g., an anti-racist organisation, is filtered down and embedded throughout the management structure. If this is not the case, there is the potential for individuals who hold negative views about sections of society to continue unchallenged. This could result in an organisation being blinded to cultural and diversity awareness, impacting career progression opportunities, recruitment, and retention for underrepresented workers in the organisation.

In the decades of working in the public and private sector, I have never had a black line manager but have experienced leadership of black female senior managers on two occasions which is a sobering and uninspiring statistic. However, I have experienced having supportive managers over the years.

One of the positive experiences was while I working as a team manager for an authority, who appointed a black female as interim head of service. During her time in the organisation, her leadership was dynamic, engaging, and inspiring. Seeing someone who looked like me who I could identify with was so inspiring and although a few years ago, I can still remember the positive effect she had on me. I am curious about her career journey and regret not being bold enough to approach her, so a missed opportunity.

Positive role models in the workplace and our personal life are of huge importance as it instils aspiration and growth in us, this is amplified when the role model looks like you. The danger for organisations is the lack of black workers occupying management and senior leadership roles. This can send the message of a lack of confidence or complacency and for black workers to be overlooked for career progression. This could also portray the organisation in a negative light to potential future black and ethnic applicants, however, the lack of diversity, could be seen as a challenge to effect change.

Black workers are disproportionally under-represented in management and senior leadership roles, and a display of the figures which underpin this can be seen below:

Black employees hold just 1.5 per cent of senior roles, research reveals. *22 June 2020 By Siobhan Palmer - https://www.peoplemanagement.co.uk/news/articles/black-employees-hold-just-1-5-per-cent-of-senior-roles*

Proportion of black individuals in the top jobs in UK business has increased by 0.1 percentage points since 2014, and remained static in the public sector black employees hold just 1.5 per cent of top management roles in the UK private sector, research has found; a figure that has increased just 0.1 percentage points since 2014.

A Business in the Community (BITC) report, **Race at the Top: Revisited***, found just 54,900 of the 3.9 million managers, directors and senior officials in the UK are black.*

According to the report, there has been even less progress on black representation in the public sector, where the number of black employees in leadership roles remained static at 1 per cent over the same period.

It found just 1 per cent of the police force across England and Wales identified as black African or black Caribbean, and none of the 39 appeal court judges in England and Wales were black.

The proportion of top private sector roles held by employees with Black, Asian and Ethnic Minority (BAME) backgrounds has increased by little over 1 percentage point, rising from 9.2 per cent of all senior positions in 2014 to 10.3 per cent today.

Sandra Kerr, race director at BITC, said the figures made clear black people continued to be under-represented at a senior level. She added that "lack of diverse leadership has a direct impact on decision-making".

Employment by Occupation – GOV.UK Ethnicity Facts and Figures Published May 2020

https://www.ethnicity-facts-figures.service.gov.uk/work-pay-and-benefits/employment/employment-by-occupation/latest

Percentage of workers in each ethnic group employed in different types of occupation.

Location United Kingdom, Time period 2018, source Annual population survey 2018.

Managers, Directors and Senior Official

All 11%

Asian 10%

Indian 11%

Pakistani/Bangladeshi 8%

Asian Other 9%

Black 5%

Mixed 9%

White 11%

White British 11%

White Other 10%

Other 10%

Summary

The Black ethnic group had the lowest percentage of workers in 'manager, director or senior official' jobs (5%).

I have spoken and listened to the experiences of black female and male individuals regarding career progression opportunities to management and senior leadership roles. The consensus in their responses was that they did not feel they had a fair opportunity to progress within their organisations, even though they felt they had the required experience, knowledge, and qualifications for the position.

Although, a scientific study was not conducted on the views of the black people I spoke with, in my opinion, the informal conversations were a good starting point in understanding their perspectives on the impact of inequality on their lives.

Delegates who represented a wide geographic spectrum of UK, were invited to share their workplace experiences to the audience of a National Black Member's Conference. There were similarities in the experiences shared, with the main theme being the feeling of being treated unfairly. The delegates shared that following an interview they often received feedback like, "You were a close second." "Keep applying for promotion." "With your experience and knowledge, you should be going for promotion." "It's a shame because we know you can do the job." Further similarities in workplace experiences shared by delegates, was that they felt that they had to work harder than their white colleagues to achieve the same recognition from employers.

It was uncanny, as some of the comments in the feedback, also resonated with me, as I had received similar feedback following unsuccessful interviews. However, I left the conference with some optimism, although the experiences shared were not easy to hear, there was a strength in solidarity to achieve our shared goal of equality.

I think it is relevant to mention the subject of figureheads, as it is an experience some may have encountered within their workplace. It is helpful to look at the use of figureheads in an organisation that lacks diversity, as they could be used in a manner that is not truly committed to equality. For example, the diverse workforce may be asked to undertake tasks that hold little leverage.

Figureheads

The quote below was researched but the source is unknown:

A figurehead is someone who appears to be in charge, but who really holds very little influence. While an organisation using a manager as a figurehead to motive and lead their team to achieve good results for the organisation another use of a figurehead could be where an organisation does not have a diverse workforce and uses a member of the diverse staff group to undertake tasks which on the surface could show respect or value to the individual but in reality, there is control over the level responsibility or influence. However, the perception of this practice could be seen as the organisation being positively promoting diversity where in reality is the contrary.

In my role as a manager the expectation of my employer is to motivate my team and achieve good results. However, learning of the other uses of figureheads in organisations is disingenuous and worrying. It can only be positive to raise awareness that there is a potential for black workers to be involved in this practice. Clearly, I would be disappointed if I unknowingly have ever been involved in the practice described above.

The quote below shows the harm and impact when uninformed assumptions are made in the workplace.

In one of the few studies that have systematically explored the perspectives of black women social workers, participants described how organisational barriers thwart their aspirations to managerial positions (Lewis, 1996). In particular, they highlighted that they have significant barriers to navigate to achieve senior positions and that the organisational climate was an influential factor in their confidence (Op. cit). They contend that a major barrier lies in deficit-informed presumptions made by managers who undervalue the skills and attributes that they bring, and often have low expectations of them so some were reluctant to put themselves forward for promotion to managerial positions as they felt they were often overlooked and essentially encountered a glass ceiling (Ibid).

Attention needs to be paid to how subtle barriers and unconscious bias may hold back black and minority ethnic workers. In particular, it is important for managers to be aware of and acknowledge the ways in which implicit racial bias may affect how judgements about suitability are made. Taking all these factors into consideration will make senior leaders better placed to understand how racism may be embedded within their processes and procedures (PM Editorial, 2020). Understanding how these factors impact the lived experiences of black and minority ethnic social workers is therefore crucial for the genuine engagement required to begin to break down these barriers.

Research in Practice: Addressing barriers to the progression of black and minority ethnic social workers to senior leadership roles.

In writing the book, it is important to also highlight the underrepresented groups who can also be impacted by unconscious bias and also overlooked in career progression opportunities - disability, gender, age, and LGBTQ+. Below are experiences gained from talking to female LGBTQ+ workers, to gain their perspective on the impact of unconscious bias on their lives:

Example 1

One of the managers that I managed was homophobic, it was difficult to prove at the time, but the person's dislike of me meant they could never truly engage with me, and always questioned me and undermined what I asked.

The main thing I could see was this person stiffening if I ever mentioned LGBT.

They then misused delegated responsibilities to create a false impression of me with superior managers and stirred up a picture of incompetence with my own teams. I did have sufficient evidence from my own line manager at the time to have acted had I felt more confident and certainly later gained information from some of my former managers to know that this wasn't a figment of my imagination. It ended up costing me promotion, credibility, and finally my job.

The reason I'd say it was unconscious bias is that this person would have felt that they acted on how they perceived me, rather than that I was a lesbian woman. What their bias did, however, was to prevent them to ever see me with an unblinkered view, and prevented any chance of acceptance or equality.

Example 2

Fairly often when I mention I have a partner when in conversation with somebody I don't know well, the person often assumes that my partner is a man or my husband. Whether this assumption is based on my physical appearance or linked to other assumptions either conscious or unconscious such as heteronormality, I don't know.

Example 3

I noticed the gender pay gap once I became a mum, my carer stalled with working part-time, I noticed changes in colleagues to my new working pattern and comments from colleagues when leaving work having worked my allotted hours! I became less skilled and qualified than men who work full time and gained promotion.

During writing the book, the UK saw images in the media, of the horrific and tragic death of a black man called George Floyd in the USA. A video of his death at the hands of the police was abhorrent and sparked huge support for the Black Lives Matter movement in the UK and around the world. The death of Mr Floyd shone the light on racism experienced by black people. I believe the death of Mr Floyd, galvanised demand for change in the UK. It was probably the catalyst for some organisations to commence engagement with diverse employees and review their vision of equality in the workplace.

Black Lives Matter protests occurred around the UK and it was heartening to see the huge diverse support by all sections of society, who attended to show their solidarity. There has been some backlash from sections of the UK, who sadly appeared to miss the point of the Black Lives Matter movement, by voicing that “all lives matter”. Clearly, all lives do matter, but until black people are treated as equals to their white counterparts, it is not possible to move forward with all lives matter.

At the time of the protests, the UK and the rest of the world was and still is (at the time of writing the book), living with the impact of the COVID-19 pandemic, which has placed restrictions on the way we live our lives. The COVID-19 pandemic highlighted the disproportional deaths in the black community, which words cannot express the sadness in hearing this. There will inevitably be the required review to understand why the black sector was affected disproportionality by the virus. However, some possible factors include low income, types of occupation and accommodation, whatever the reason the impact on the black community is a further concern regarding inequality.

Over the decades, having limited role models in organisations that I have worked in have impacted me more than I probably acknowledged. Seeing female leaders who I can identify with provides me with a sense of pride and paves the way for others to follow. It is certainly not my intention to portray myself as not having aspirations, but sometimes, despite experience, knowledge, qualifications, and working hard, it is not enough to penetrate the glass ceiling.

There is, I believe justification in saying unconscious bias has had some influence regarding the lack of diverse sectors of the organisations in management roles. Clearly, geographics could also be a factor, but having worked in inner cities and rural locations, seeing black people in leadership and management roles is lacking.

Chapter 3
The power in changing perspectives

"Change will not come if we wait for some other person or some other time. We are the ones we've been waiting for. We are the change that we seek."

Barack Obama

This chapter aims to acknowledge that in some organisations, steps may have taken place to address the disparity in the progression of black workers, but for many organisations, there is still a lot of work to do. The government statistics mentioned in chapter two state that the Black ethnic group had the lowest percentage of workers in ‘manager, director or senior official’ jobs (5%). Thus, all of our efforts and planning will need to be focused on the address and work to improve this percentage. Barrack Obama’s inspirational quote mentioned above is absolutely correct and we have to use our voice as the instigator for change.

Below are my thoughts on what should be in place in the work setting, to effect positive change from the perspective of the employee and employer. The suggestions are measures, which in my opinion should enable equal opportunities. They are not intended to be exhaustive.

Measures to assist in developing and implementing equal career opportunities in the organisation:

Employer responsibility to progress:

- Career progression policy.
  Do you have a career progression plan which is reviewed in a timely manner?
- Annual performance employee scheme.
- Secondment opportunities.
- Shadowing opportunities to enable upskilling.

- The organisation's data collection, on the number of black workers in the organisation, compared to the diversity in the geographic area. Data showing black worker's retention data, progression to management roles and pay inequalities.

  Do you have access to the data above, do you know the organisation's strategic plan/ timeframe to improve data findings and how is this monitored?
- Recruitment and retention policy, including diverse interview panels.
- Training which offers interview techniques.

  Who monitors and hold the organisation to account if interviews held do not have a diverse panel?

- Anti-Racism policy.

  Anti-Racism and unconscious bias training, is the training mandatory for everyone in the organisation?
- Human resources collaboration with stakeholders to ensure policy and procedures are reviewed and current.
- Supervision/ 1:1 policy.

  Access to regular planned and recorded supervision/1:1 session.
- Mentor/Buddy scheme.

  If not in place, consider who you need to approach to set up a mentor/buddy scheme?
- Reverse mentoring.
- Coaching opportunity.

If not in place, consider who you need to approach to gain access to a coach.

- Talent pool scheme.
- Black worker's staff group, also a mechanism to review policy/ procedure to influence change.

  If not in place, work in collaboration with black colleagues and senior leaders to implement a staff group.
- Peer support from a comparator organisation to review diversity vision and embeddedness.

Employee:

The perspective for the employee, in my opinion, should mirror the points suggested above for the employer. It is the responsibility of the employer to ensure equal opportunity infrastructure is in place to benefit all employees. The aim of the suggested measures is to assist the employee with things they can do, to hold the employer to account if the measures above are not in place. The text in bold highlights further prompts for the employee.

The suggested measures aim to help the organisation create a culturally aware environment where employees feel valued, respected, and it is evident to them that the employer is committed to an equal workforce. Utilising the skills already available and a template of opportunities for employees to grow and excel can only be of benefit to the culture of the organisation.

These measures, in my opinion, should have a positive impact on staff retention, as there is scope for the employee to map career progression. This can also benefit the reputation of the organisation in how it is perceived by future applicants of an organisation who has a clear vision on career opportunities of their diverse workforce.

As a member of a professional body or trade union can also provide information on career development, training opportunities and accessible support regarding potential issues in the workplace, including awareness of the Equality Act 2010.

The power to change perspectives, for both the employee and employer, is uplifting. In the previous chapters, examples of lived experiences that raise questions of fairness and the message to employers, are, we have talked about inequalities for too long, what is required now is action to enable change.

During the journey of writing the book, as mentioned, the death of George Floyd has galvanised the momentum for change. The action for change within the workplace, need to commence with the solidarity and support from non-black colleagues. The allyship of non-black colleagues is important in calling out the microaggression and racism they witness. The impetus, in the fight to combat unconscious bias, is a responsibility for all.

Microaggression - a subtle but offensive comment or action directed at a member of a marginalised group, especially a racial minority, that is often unintentionally offensive or unconsciously reinforces a stereotype (Dictionary.com).

The benefits of a coach relayed by a friend helped discussion around career development and suggestions to help achieve her goals. These benefits have also been echoed during conversations with senior managers while researching the book. If organisations do not have mentors in place, it is something I think should seriously be considered to help, provide guidance, motivation, and role modelling. Having a mentor, I could identify with, is important and something I should have contemplated earlier. It is also worth considering accessing a mentor outside one's place of work.

Through researching for the book, I was made aware of positive changes that have taken place within the fire service, on the issue of cultural competence. The structure of the senior leaders within the organisation are predominantly white, middle-aged males. The solutions implemented within the organisation were to have open discussions about bias to recognise that people in the organisation were not bad people. It was important for the organisation through its work to understand where the bias came from to help positive changes going forward.

The workers within the organisation were said to be open and honest and recognised issues of white privilege (*the fact of people with white skin having advantages in society that other people do not have (Cambridge dictionary 2019*)), which were not considered previously but was now better understood. The service brought in training to upskill on issues of unconscious bias. This example of efforts to change the culture within the organisation demonstrates that being open to reflect on your practice and beliefs can be powerful in effecting change. It will be wrong to assume that there is no work to do within the fire service regarding career progression opportunities for their diverse workforce, but it is important to acknowledge the positive steps that have been taken so far.

Another positive example of the progress being made was in the Travel

Industry. Similar to the fire service, the leadership team were predominately white. But positively, the number of black employees at entry-level were close to the number of black people in the national working average. However, there was a disproportionately; lack of black line managers and leaders. Here, an example of reverse mentoring and leaders' sponsorship used to help combat disparities.

Reverse mentoring is a mentoring relationship between a junior employee and a more senior employee, in which the senior employee is mentored. Here a safe space is created in which the junior employee educates and mentors the Director on issues that people who are ethnic minorities face in day-to-day working life.

In the beginning, the partnership may feel uncomfortable, if it is, the first conversation about race in the workplace, which the Director had participated in with a black person. However, there are great opportunities for growth and tangible action to be created from the partnership. Furthermore, the reverse mentoring relationship benefits the junior employee, they have an advocate in the management of their company and naturally learn from the experience of the Director.

Reverse mentoring differs from executive sponsorship, mentoring or coaching because there is a real focus on the junior employee leading the conversation about their experiences. The employee also shares positive experiences, utilising the sponsorship from the leadership team.

By assigning members of leadership to sponsor the company's Diversity and Inclusion strategy and employees, it provides accountability and advocacy. Furthermore, the increased conversations between the executive sponsors and black employees; help black employees build a positive network in the company.

For positive change to happen with black workers progressing to middle and senior management roles, organisations will need to consider why this is not happening to enable change in the status quo. The reason there is such a disparity in black workers not occupying senior roles, in my opinion, is not because they do not have the expertise, knowledge, or qualification. They will undoubtedly offer a different perspective and provide fresh ideas which may constructively challenge how things are done in the organisation.

Change will occur with organisations' commitment to ensuring that there are an equal number of black workers to white colleagues at all levels of management progression. Recognition of the benefits of a diverse workforce should be embraced, not feared, and implemented with impetus.

CONCLUSION

Writing this book has been a cathartic experience and provided space to reflect and address issues that are passionate to me in an open and honest way.

I suppose there are two aspects to the book in approaching the subject of the unconscious, the first is the impact on the daily lives of individuals and the second is whether there is a correlation between unconscious bias on career progression of black workers. If the outcome is that there is no correlation, we will need to consider what explanation can be provided, to the statistics presented in chapter 2 which states that the *Black ethnic group had the lowest percentage of workers in 'manager, director or senior official' jobs (5%).*

My view is that unconscious bias can influence the recruitment process and that's why it is crucial to have the necessary checks and balances in place to counter this. The vision of the organisation to have a diverse workforce and how the vision is embedded is fundamental in ensuring equal opportunities is part of its everyday activities. We have seen examples in the book where there are situations where it is not always obvious to some that they are displaying biases, so organisations need to ensure that whole staffing groups are culturally aware.

The aim of writing the book was for it to be of value to both employees and employers. I hope that following reading this book, as an employer you will have found the content helpful and informative to assist with changes you consider necessary. To the employee, following reading the book, I hope it has re-energised you to push for the career progression that you may have been undecided to pursue.

The ability to achieve one's aspirations and goals in life should be available to everyone, and by continuing to raise our voices in echoing this message, we will bring about change and equality for all.

The focus of the book has been the impact of unconscious bias on black workers, but as highlighted in the book, people subjected to protected characteristics are also impacted by unconscious bias and thus I hope that the content will be beneficial in their fight for equality.

Examples presented in the book show the experiences of exposure to unconscious bias, however, we need to be mindful that some biases are conscious. It is the responsibility of everyone to challenge these negative behaviours whenever confronted with them, with a collective aim of living together in an anti-racist society.

As mentioned earlier, the death of George Floyd, reignited the issues of inequalities and has brought them to the forefront of our minds. The Black Lives Matter protests held, displayed heart-warming solidarity, from diverse sectors of society to support the cause. Inequalities affect many aspects of our life and are not reserved for the workplace. It is important that the momentum remains focused on the issue and not derailed by the media or by politicians, being side-tracked, e.g., the removal of monuments or whether 'the knee' should be taken.

The challenge and difficult conversations in moving this matter forward cannot be underestimated. There is the likelihood that there will be situations where defensiveness occurs, levelled at those of us raising the issue. I think it is important that conversations are not based on blame but used as an opportunity for learning and effect change in behaviour and thoughts.

We have heard the positive steps taken by some organisations to combat unconscious bias who have equal opportunities schemes to acknowledge the talent, this is very encouraging.

The aim of the research for this book was always to capture the experiences of a wide range of individuals at differing levels, different geographical locations, and different organisations to provide objectivity and true reflection in presenting the issues.

Finally, having a diverse workforce provides different perspectives which incorporate a wealth of different lived experiences and ideas, which in my opinion, is a strength and demonstrates the organisation's inclusivity.

In a small way, the hope is that the book has helped individuals to continue to believe in their aspirations and feel more equipped to not allow anyone to limit or cap their ability or ambition, and make, breaking through the glass ceiling their reality.

"Never be limited by other people's limited imaginations. If you adopt their attitudes, then the possibility won't exist because you'll have already shut it out…You can hear other people's wisdom, but you've got to re-evaluate the world for yourself."

- Mae Jemison

REFERENCES

Alexander, C. & Arday, J. (eds) (2015) Aiming Higher: Race, Inequality and Diversity in the Academy. London: Runnymede Trust. Available at: http://www.runnymedetrust.org/uploads/ Aiming%20 Higher.pdf

Banaji, M.R. & Greenwald, A.G. (2013). *Blindspot: Hidden biases of good people*. New York, NY: Delacorte Press

Bellack, J.P.(2015. Unconscious Bias: An Obstacle to Cultural Competence. *Journal of Nursing Education*, 54(9), pp.S63-S64. https://doi.org/10.3928/01484834-20150814-12

Black employees hold just 1.5 per cent of senior roles, research reveals (2020). *Black employees hold just 1.5 per cent of senior roles, research reveals*. [online] People Management. Available at: https://www.peoplemanagement.co.uk/news/articles/black-employees-hold-just-1-5-per-cent-of-senior-roles.

Business in the Community. (n.d.). *Black livelihoods matter: Less than 2% of top management roles are held by black employees*. [online] Available at: https://www.bitc.org.uk/news/black-livelihoods-matter-less-than-2-in-top-management-roles-are-black/.

Cambridge Dictionary (2019). *WHITE PRIVILEGE | meaning in the Cambridge English Dictionary*. [online] Cambridge.org. Available at: https://dictionary.cambridge.org/dictionary/english/white-privilege.

Dictionary.com. (n.d.). *Definition of micro-aggression*. [online] Available at: https://www.dictionary.com/browse/microaggression.

Funded by the Department for Education PSDP -Resources for Managers of Practice Supervisors. (n.d.). [online] . Available at: https://practice-supervisors.rip.org.uk/wp-content/uploads/2021/01/StS_KB_Addressing_Barriers_Progression_of_Black_and_Minority_Ethnic_SWs_FINAL.pdf.

Ives Erikson, J. (2015, February5). Blind spot: Do unconscious biases affect our hiring, firing, work relationships, and the care we provide? *Caring Headlines*, pp. 2–3. Retrieved from http://www.mghpcs.org/news/caringheadlines/Documents/2015/February_5_2015.pdf

The Black Curriculum. (n.d.). *The Black Curriculum*. [online] Available at: https://theblackcurriculm.com. United Kingdom (2018). *Employment by occupation*. [online] Service.gov.uk. Available at: https://www.ethnicity-facts-figures.service.gov.uk/work-pay-and-benefits/employment/employment-by-occupation/latest.

www.contributoria.com. (n.d.). *Saving money the Jamaican way – the "Paadna" as an alternative to the high street bank :*

July 2014 : Contributoria - people supporting journalism. [online] Available at: http://www.contributoria.com/issue/2014-07/537111f530d0f1ab0f000010.html

NOTES

NOTES

Printed in Great Britain
by Amazon

71514867R10058